bury the dead

OMBS, CORPSES, MUMMIES, SKELETONS, & RITUALS

BY CHRISTOPHER SLOAN

FOREWORD BY DR. BRUNO FROHLICH,
SMITHSONIAN INSTITUTION

SCHOLASTIC INC.

New York Toronto London Auckland Sydney
Mexico City New Delhi Hong Kong Buenos Aires

John M. Fahey
*President and
Chief Executive Officer*

Gilbert M. Grosvenor
Chairman of the Board

Nina D. Hoffman
*Executive Vice President and
President, Books and
School Publishing*

Staff for this book

Nancy Laties Feresten
*Vice President and
Editor-in-Chief, Children's Books
Project Editor*

Jo H. Tunstall
Assistant Editor

Bea Jackson
Art Director, Children's Books

Lewis R. Bassford
Production Manager

Jim Enzinna
Indexer

*Illustrations and permissions: Portia Sloan
Design by Christopher Sloan*

Principal consultants

Dr. Bruno Frohlich
Smithsonian Institution

Dr. Michael Parker Pearson
University of Sheffield

Linda Goldman, MS
*Certified Grief Therapist and
Certified Grief Educator*

First Burials: Dr. Fred Smith
Northern Illinois University

Egypt: Dr. Mark Lehner
*Oriental Institute,
University of Chicago*

Scytho-Siberians:
Dr. Esther Jacobson
University of Oregon

China: Dr. Jeffrey Riegel
University of California, Berkeley

Moche: Dr. Christopher Donnan
University of California, Los Angeles

Acknowledgments

The inspiration for this book came from the beautiful archaeological art and photography published by the National Geographic Society over the years. To the artists, photographers, and editors who created that body of work, I owe thanks. I am particularly indebted to Ken Garrett and Lou Mazzatenta for their excellent photos. Dr. Chris Donnan, Dr. Bruno Frohlich, Dr. Mark Kenoyer, and Dr. Fred Wendorf were also kind enough to let me use photographs from their archaeological fieldwork. The assistance of Joergen Birman, Jill Burch, Emily Krieger, Adam Schaeffer, and Portia Sloan in collecting images for this book was indispensable.

Comments on the text from Portia Sloan, Jessica Sloan, and the terrific editors at the National Geographic Children's Book Division were insightful and invaluable.

The expert review of the book by the consultants listed at left, however, is what makes it special. Despite their busy schedules of teaching, researching, and traveling around the world to do their work, they were all enthusiastic about helping with a children's book on this subject. In the course of this project, they stayed in touch whether they were in the United States, the United Kingdom, Peru, or Thailand.

Cover: *One of the world's earliest known mummies from the Chinchorro culture of Chile.*
Title page: *A stark image of death from a tombstone in the floor of the Roskilde Cathedral in Denmark, where many kings, queens, and nobles have been buried since the 15th century.*

One of the world's largest nonprofit scientific and educational organizations, the National Geographic Society was founded in 1888 "for the increase and diffusion of geographic knowledge." Fulfilling this mission, the Society educates and inspires millions every day through its magazines, books, television programs, videos, maps and atlases, research grants, the National Geographic Bee, teacher workshops, and innovative classroom materials. The Society is supported through membership dues, charitable gifts, and income from the sale of its educational products. This support is vital to National Geographic's mission to increase global understanding and promote conservation of our planet through exploration, research, and education.

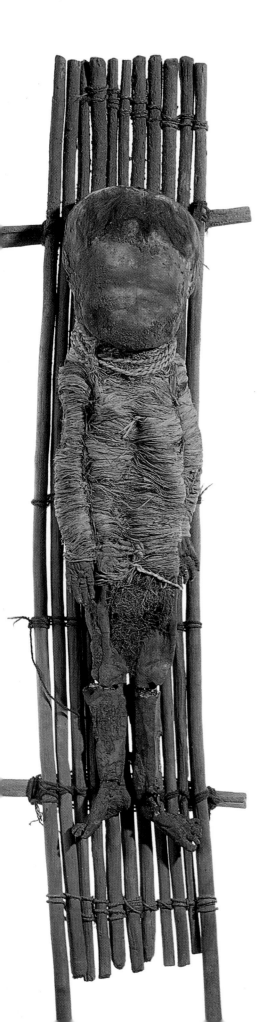

Contents

The world's earliest known mummy makers, the Chinchorro people, lived on the dry coast of Chile around 7,000 years ago. Their mummies, including the child (far left) and the fetus (above, center), were often buried with small wooden dolls that looked like real mummies.

Foreword

Until recently, some newborn infants that died in the Aleutian Islands of the North Pacific (below) were artificially mummified by removing some of the body's organs and replacing them with dried grass. The body would be wrapped in bird skin, sea-mammal fur, and grass matting, then placed in a woven backpack (above). Mothers would carry them for weeks or months, communicating with the infant's spirit until it was ready for burial and to go on to another world.

The history of how people have viewed death and treated the dead is intensely interesting to me as an archaeologist. Death is one of the great mysteries, so different cultures explain it differently and make different choices about how to care for a loved one's body after death. We can see tremendous variety in funeral practices even in our own times, and we can learn a lot about the lives of prehistoric peoples by studying their tombs and by comparing what we find there to what we know about present-day life and burial customs.

In *Bury the Dead,* Christopher Sloan describes how people in rich and diverse cultures, ancient and modern-day, bury their dead. He focuses on a small group of well-documented examples for Europe, Africa, Asia, and the Americas, showing how studying a culture's burial practices helps archaeologists like me learn about the lives of those cultures.

I have spent my whole working life teasing the secrets of ancient cultures from tombs and burials, so I'm very pleased to be associated with a book that brings such excitement and depth of information about the subject to young people.

DR. BRUNO FROHLICH
National Museum of Natural History, Smithsonian Institution

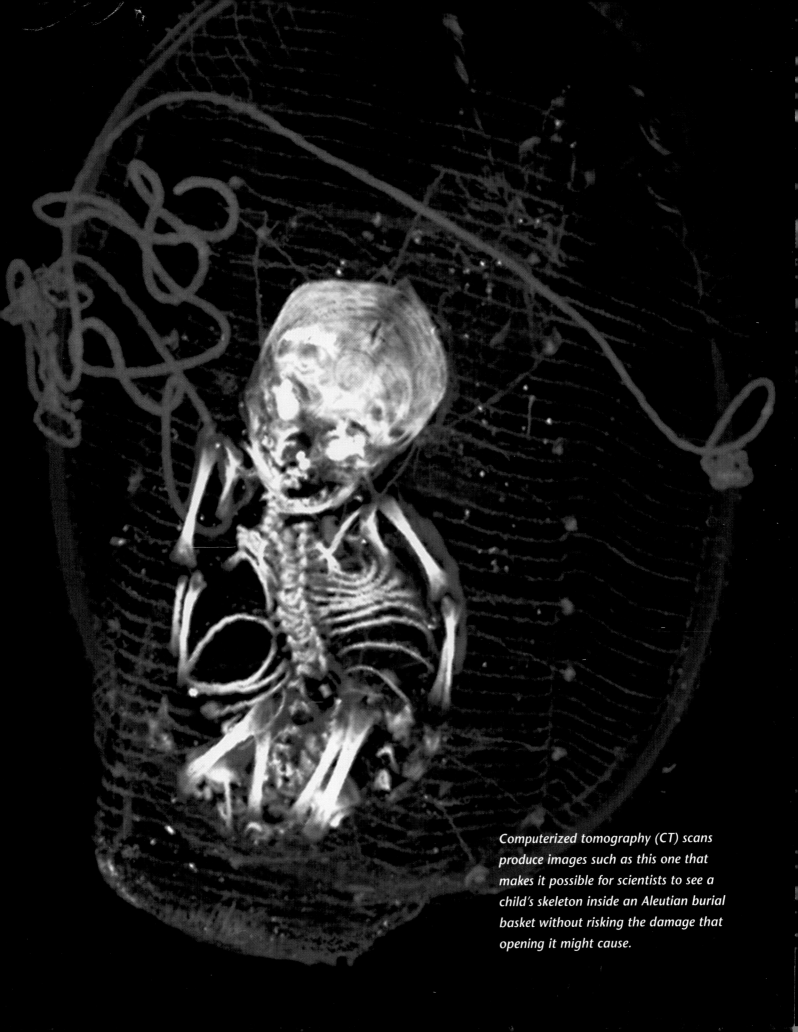

Computerized tomography (CT) scans produce images such as this one that makes it possible for scientists to see a child's skeleton inside an Aleutian burial basket without risking the damage that opening it might cause.

Why People Bury Their Dead

A Chacopoya mummy stares out from under a burial cloth that wrapped it for centuries in its tomb. The burials of these pre-Inca Peruvians are among the most inaccessible on Earth. They perch on the sides of cliffs and can only be reached by skilled climbers.

The Chacopoya buried their dead on the sides of cliffs that erupt out of the green jungles of Peru. The people of Pazyryk in Siberia stuffed fur in place of the eyeballs and straw in place of the brains of those who died. The ancient Chinese covered their dead royalty head to toe in suits of jade.

From our point of view in the 21st century, ancient burials may seem strange, but so may many funeral activities being practiced around the world today. For example, babies are buried in trees on the island of Sulawesi in Indonesia; bodies are fed to vultures and other birds in Tibet; and in the Amazon rain forest, the Yanomami dead are burned, crushed, and then eaten.

North Americans and Europeans shop for coffins as we would for cars and buy and sell grave plots in cemeteries. The United States is one of the only countries in the world to regularly embalm the dead. Embalming is a way of artificially preserving a corpse. During modern embalming, every drop of blood is drained out of a corpse's veins, and a preservative that keeps the body from rotting away is pumped in to replace it.

Humans have always had a wide variety of death-related activities, and those of today are echoes of the many different burial customs that people have practiced over the last 100,000 years or so. That is why archaeologists—scientists who study past cultures—are interested in the reasons why we bury the dead the way we do. It helps them understand burials (and cultures) of the past.

The variety of burial practices past and present is due to different beliefs about what happens after death. Some cultures compare death to sleeping. For example, the tombstone inscription "R.I.P." comes from the latin *requiescant in pace* or "may

Kings, queens, and other rich or famous people are buried in the walls and under the floors of Westminster Abbey in London, England (above). Many Christians believe that burial within or near churches is a way to be closer to God in the afterlife. People on the island of Sulawesi in Indonesia bury infants in a tree (right) for similar reasons. They believe the child will rise up safely to the heavens through the trunk.

they rest in peace." Others believe that we will experience a different kind of life after death. This existence after death often takes place in a spirit world sometimes called the afterlife.

Beliefs about life after death have led to special death-related activities called funerary rituals. These customs are performed at the time of death and can last for years. Today, for example, many Europeans and North Americans wear black when mourning and put flowers or small gifts on graves year after year.

These customs help people work through the grief that death can bring to a community. Some, such as the gathering of mourners in some Irish and African-American communities, called a wake, provide comfort by celebrating the life of the dead. Funerary rituals can include spontaneous expressions of grief, too. After the sudden death of Princess Diana of the United Kingdom and after the destruction of the World Trade Center towers in New York City, people left flowers, gifts, and messages to the dead in public areas. Providing items for the departed is a way of saying good-bye and showing respect for the dead, but it is also a way to help the living cope with their grief. These rituals make us feel that we are somehow still taking care of our lost loved ones. In the same way, rituals that ask supernatural forces to assist the dead also help the living feel better.

People in almost all cultures are afraid of the dead. Horror stories of vampires, ghosts, and ghouls help us express such fears. Fear of the dead is one reason why funerary rituals are often designed to separate the dead from the living. In Europe and North America we bury people six feet underground. The Iban people of Borneo have another way of creating distance. They believe that they can cut ties with the deceased by burying a knife with each corpse.

Many people are fearful of ancestors and restless spirits. To prevent a person's spirit from haunting them, Zulu men in South Africa walk backward while carrying the body to its grave.

The Maya, a civilization that lived in Mesoamerica from 1000 B.C. to A.D. 900, buried their royalty in tombs that were part of great ceremonial centers. These centers consisted of pyramids and large plazas. Burials discovered within these structures show that pyramids often contained multiple burials. The earliest burials were built over by succeeding generations, making each pyramid a complex puzzle. In this scene the body of a Maya ruler is being sealed into a chamber along with grave goods, including food and clothing, for his life after death.

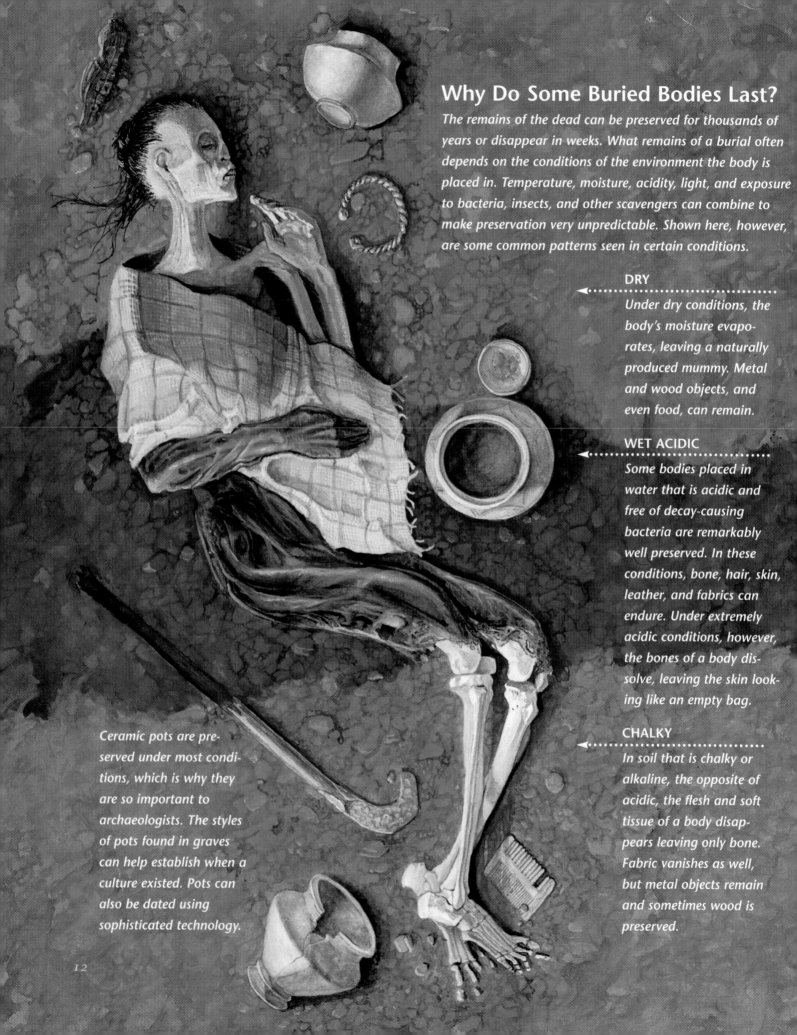

Why Do Some Buried Bodies Last?

The remains of the dead can be preserved for thousands of years or disappear in weeks. What remains of a burial often depends on the conditions of the environment the body is placed in. Temperature, moisture, acidity, light, and exposure to bacteria, insects, and other scavengers can combine to make preservation very unpredictable. Shown here, however, are some common patterns seen in certain conditions.

DRY

Under dry conditions, the body's moisture evaporates, leaving a naturally produced mummy. Metal and wood objects, and even food, can remain.

WET ACIDIC

Some bodies placed in water that is acidic and free of decay-causing bacteria are remarkably well preserved. In these conditions, bone, hair, skin, leather, and fabrics can endure. Under extremely acidic conditions, however, the bones of a body dissolve, leaving the skin looking like an empty bag.

CHALKY

In soil that is chalky or alkaline, the opposite of acidic, the flesh and soft tissue of a body disappears leaving only bone. Fabric vanishes as well, but metal objects remain and sometimes wood is preserved.

Ceramic pots are preserved under most conditions, which is why they are so important to archaeologists. The styles of pots found in graves can help establish when a culture existed. Pots can also be dated using sophisticated technology.

They believe this will confuse the spirit of the dead so it cannot find its way back to haunt the living. Many East Asian cultures believe that tending the graves of their ancestors by weeding or sweeping and making frequent offerings will keep the dead content so they will not come back as ghosts or vampires to make trouble.

Vampires and ghouls are creatures of the imagination, but there are real reasons to be afraid. Death causes bodies to change in unpleasant and sometimes dangerous ways. A few minutes after death, the skin begins to blotch with red and purple patches in a condition called *livor mortis*. After several hours, *rigor mortis* sets in and the body stiffens, only to relax again hours later. Decay sets in after a couple of days, turning the skin a greenish color and causing a bad smell. Dead bodies can carry disease, cause infection, and attract swarms of disease-carrying insects and scavengers. This makes disposal of a dead body a necessary thing.

Some scientists have suggested that human burials started with the need to dispose of decaying corpses. Others argue that there was more to it. They suggest that early burials were the first sign of spiritual thinking in humans. They point to the careful placement of bodies and to items left in graves—called grave goods—as providing comfort and protection for the dead in an afterlife. We may never know if either of these views is correct, but scientists agree that the origin of human burials is probably linked to the origins of being truly human.

Each burial is like a window into the past. Sometimes we can see a lot of what an ancient culture was like from the ruins of towns, temples, and workshops, and from their writings. Yet often all that remains is what was left in graves. When they discover an ancient tomb or grave, archaeologists study every detail like detectives to gather as much information as possible. By combining their studies of ancient burials with an understanding of why and how we bury people today, archaeologists can give us a better understanding not only of the history of burials, but of humanity itself.

Many burials are carefully planned to pay respect to the dead and care for them by providing them with belongings that will be useful to them in an afterlife. This man, buried in a grave cut in chalk at Deal in England about 200 B.C., was found with a bronze crown encircling his head and an iron sword by his side.

The First Burials

Stones fill the eye sockets of the skull of a Cro-Magnon girl found in a French cave called Mas-d'Azil. Ice Age burials like this one show that the first modern humans to arrive in Europe between 35,000 and 40,000 years ago were caring for their dead in ways that no one had before.

Who was the first person ever buried? We do not know, but at some point in the distant past, our ancestors started taking care of each other, and part of that care included burial. The sick were nursed until they healed, the elderly were supported in their old age, and those who died were thoughtfully buried.

The first evidence that people supported the sick and elderly is clearly seen in bones that are around 60,000 years old. These bones show breaks and infections that had healed as well as crippling bone diseases such as arthritis that people had lived with for many years. These injuries and diseases would have prevented people from caring for themselves. Because they survived, we know they must have been cared for by others.

It is hard to say when burial with care began. This is because it is difficult for archaeologists to tell the difference between a corpse buried in a cave as part of a funerary ritual and one buried there to get rid of the smell. Clues from several sites where bones of early humans were found, however, show signs of how the first thoughtful burials might look different from just throwing a body away.

Deep within a cave called La Sima de los Huesos (the Pit of the Bones) in the Sierra Atapuerca, a group of hills in Spain, lies what may be the earliest example of caring burials. There, at the bottom of a 40-foot-deep hole, is a pile of bones. It is made up of the skeletons of at least 32 early humans mixed in with a number of bear skeletons. They died about 300,000 years ago.

It's hard to be sure that the people in the Pit of the Bones were buried. Perhaps those bones came together in another way. The people could have been eaten by animals that lived in the cave or they could have been living in the cave when it collapsed and trapped them. Or the pit could have been a garbage dump where ancient people threw away any kind of garbage, including dead bodies.

Scientists working on the site do not see evidence for these explanations. The bones of bodies eaten by animals should show bite marks, but these bones have none. And this collection of bones is larger than animals usually make. If the people had been living in the cave, we would expect to find stone tools, weapons, or the remains of fireplaces. The Pit of the Bones had none of these. There is no sign of other trash in the pit. This leaves the thoughtful placement of dead bodies in the pit as the best explanation for what happened. But of course, we will never be sure.

Though we may never know if the early humans of the Pit of the Bones performed rituals for their dead, we can be pretty sure that humans that came later did. These include Neandertals and early modern humans.

The Neandertals lived in an area that stretched from Spain to Uzbekistan about 230,000 to 27,000 years ago. They are best known for their big brows, big brains (bigger than ours!), large noses, and stout bodies. Archaeologists have found many Neandertal bodies in shallow pits lying on their sides with arms and legs tucked in. At Shanidar Cave, in Iraq, clumps of flower pollen were found buried in what appears to be a 60,000-year-old Neandertal grave. Since some of the pollen was from plants that could be used for medicine, it is possible that this man was not just buried with flowers but was a medicine man, or shaman.

Early modern humans came later than Neandertals, but evidence of their burials is thousands of years more ancient. Like Neandertals, they apparently laid the bodies of the dead in shallow pits. At a 115,000 year-old site called Qafzeh in Israel, an early modern human child's skeleton was found with its hand on a deer skull and antlers placed across its neck. Evidence such as this makes a strong case that early modern humans and Neandertals were providing their dead with things they would need in an afterlife.

A body plunges down a shaft into the Pit of the Bones (left), a site deep within a Spanish cave where the earliest known caring burials may have taken place. At Shanidar in Iraq, a Neandertal burial showed that a man had survived the loss of an arm and an eye and had crippling arthritis (right). All of this, plus the fact that he was found buried on his side (inset), suggests that other Neandertals may have cared for him in life as well as in death.

Cut marks on Neandertal bones found at Krapina Cave in Croatia show that cannibalism was probably practiced there. While this may seem barbaric to us at first glance, it is possible that it was part of a funerary ritual.

In several areas where the Neandertals lived, such as the caves at Krapina, in Croatia, there is evidence that points to a different sort of funerary ritual. Bones were found here with cut marks and breaks similar in pattern to those in the bones of animals that were slaughtered and then eaten. These people were probably eating their dead.

Scientists who study cannibalism find that it is not always related to hunger. Many cultures throughout history have eaten the dead as a funerary ritual. Modern-day women of the Gimi tribe in Papua New Guinea eat the flesh of deceased men so that their spirits may be free to rejoin their ancestors. The Yanomami living in the Amazon rain forest cremate their dead and then eat the ashes as a kind of mush to make sure the spirits of the deceased are not lost. Perhaps some of the Neandertals also ate their dead as a funerary ritual rather than out of hunger.

There is much evidence to suggest that early modern humans emerged from Africa about 100,000 years ago and spread around the world from there. The ones that arrived in Europe during a warm period in a great ice age between 35,000 and 40,000 years ago are particularly interesting. Their burial practices and other remains, such as cave art, show that these humans had begun to think the way we do. Archaeologists call these people the Cro-Magnons. Cro-Magnons covered corpses with bright red ocher, a pigment made from iron oxide. They placed jewelry made from animal bones, mammoth ivory, and fox teeth in their graves, and laid beautifully crafted stone tools and weapons near the deceased.

At Sunghir, a 23,000-year-old site near Moscow, Russia, archaeologist Otto N. Bader unearthed one of the most elaborate Ice Age burials ever discovered. It contained two skeletons of children placed head to head in a grave. More than 10,000 ivory beads made from mammoth tusks were arranged in patterns over their bones as though they had once been sewn on a garment that had rotted away over time. The archaeologists also found a fox-tooth belt, long ivory poles, and a polished human leg bone.

Why were these dead children so well provided for? Many scientists agree that the Sunghir burials are the earliest known signs of differences in social standing. It appears that certain people were buried with more grave goods than others. In fact, the children at Sunghir were buried with much more than an average adult would have owned in that time and place. Their burials are so different from other graves in the area that it is easy to imagine that these children were from a distinguished family. Perhaps they were the children of a powerful chief.

Two Cro-Magnon children placed head to head in a grave at Sunghir in Russia (shown above in a museum replica) were buried like royalty, with beaded garments, ivory poles, and a human thigh bone.

About 9,000 years after these Cro-Magnon children were buried in Europe, another grave site with startling contents was prepared by people in faraway Sudan, in North Africa. Here, at a 14,000-year-old site called Jebel Sahaba, Dr. Fred Wendorf discovered spear and arrow points lying among the skeletons of 59 people. Weapons had been found in graves before, but this time they were discovered actually embedded in bone. Dr. Wendorf thinks the people buried here were victims of warfare. Jebel Sahaba was drier than normal at the time, so perhaps too many people were competing for too little food. This situation can easily lead to war.

A more peaceful scene soon emerged in Southwest Asia in what are now Israel and Jordan. People were farming and settling together in permanent villages for the first time in human history. Life was even pleasant enough to allow for pets. The earliest evidence of people keeping animals as pets comes from one of these settlements where a child was buried with a puppy.

The Natufians, as archaeologists call these early villagers, lived about 12,000 years ago. They placed graves within the village and often under the floors in their own homes. Burials from 8000 B.C. show that the Natufians' descendants removed the skulls from adult skeletons and

Pencils point to arrow tips that lie among skeletons in a mass grave at Jebel Sahaba in Sudan (left), a 14,000-year-old site that shows the first evidence of warfare. In ancient Dilmun, now Bahrain, people buried their dead in 85,000 mounds that cover the landscape (above). Archaeologists benefit from studying huge gravesites like these because the information they collect allows them to get a picture of a whole population.

placed them on display in their homes. Sometimes these skulls were decorated with molded plaster faces with seashells placed in the eye sockets to look like eyes. Archaeologists interpret these skull displays and burials in houses as a sign that people wanted to keep ancestors nearby. They think this may be early evidence of ancestor worship.

As farming lifestyles emerged in different parts of the world, so did settlements, and it wasn't long before people were building villages almost everywhere. These early builders were also the first to construct monuments as a way to remember their dead. Among these were tombs made of large stone blocks called megaliths. In France and the British Isles, megaliths often weighed dozens of tons. Modern engineers still puzzle over the determination and clever methods these people must have devised, first to move these blocks and then to stand them on end more than 6,000 years ago.

As the world became more populated, centers of power grew, and so did the monuments. Huge tombs of earth and stone took the shape of mountains. The largest is the Great Pyramid of Giza in Egypt. It towers 481 feet above the desert and is made of more than two and a half million stones.

Sometimes these monumental tombs were used for one funeral and then left alone. Yet for

Time Line of Burial History

| 115,000 B.C. | 40,000 B.C. | 12,000 B.C. | 8000 B.C. | 5000 B.C. | 4000 B.C. |

The earliest human burials probably occurred among Neandertals and the earliest modern humans. Shown here is a Neandertal skull.

Modern humans arrived in Europe with new tools, art, and elaborate burial customs. Shown here are tiny beads from the clothing of a child buried in western Russia 23,000 years ago.

In Sudan, mass graves of people killed violently show that humans had started what can be described as warfare.

Archaeologists think that skulls covered in plaster and decorated with seashell eyes are some of the earliest evidence of ancestor worship. This skull is from the West Bank town of Jericho.

The world's earliest known intentionally mummified remains are from the Chinchorro culture in Chile.

Early settlers of Europe constructed huge stone tombs called megaliths. This one is near the village of West Kennet in England.

the Maya, Aztec, and mound-builder cultures in the Americas, tombs were centers of activity. These cultures opened tombs again and again—or built new layers on top of old ones—to allow many bodies to be buried at one spot. One Native American burial mound excavated in New Hampshire is estimated to contain more than 8,000 bodies.

Not all cultures piled gold into graves. Many, like the Harappans who lived in what is now Pakistan from 2600 B.C. to 1900 B.C., kept their precious metals with the living and placed other grave goods, such as these beautiful clay pots, which were once filled with food and drink, in burials instead.

The intention of most tombs was to create a place where the dead could lie undisturbed for eternity. Yet of the billions of burials throughout history, most suffered from decay. To fight this decay, people invented ways of artificially preserving bodies by drying—called mummification. The earliest known examples of mummification come from the Chinchorro culture of Chile—a people that lived in one of the driest places on Earth 7,000 years ago. Their burials involved taking the flesh off corpses and stuffing the skins with stick frames and plants. Many other cultures have experimented with mummification since then, including people from Egypt, Peru, Madagascar, Siberia, and the Canary, Aleutian, and Philippine islands.

Which ancient burials are preserved and which are not is a matter of luck. Natural conditions, which can change dramatically over time, can destroy even the finest mummy and preserve the least prepared grave. Destructive human tampering with tombs and gravesites is unpredictable as well. This makes the chance of finding undisturbed, well-preserved remains slim. When we find them, however, the reward is great. Ancient burials are one of the most important records of human history.

2500 B.C.	700 B.C.	220 B.C.	A.D. 200	A.D. 1800s	Present

| The Egyptian pyramids are among the largest tombs ever constructed. The three pyramids at Giza, one of which is shown here, were built in as little as 70 years. (See pages 24-31.) | Much of what we know about the Scythians comes from scenes created on golden objects found in their tombs. Shown here is a man having his tooth pulled. (See pages 32-39.) | Unified China's first emperor had an army of clay soldiers built to accompany him in death. Shown here is a computer-colored image of what the soldiers would have looked like when they were first buried. (See pages 40-47.) | The Moche in Peru constructed large tombs for their chieftains and dressed them in what appears to be ceremonial attire, which included objects of copper, silver, and gold. (See pages 48-55.) | In the 19th century, industrialization dramatically affected burial practices in the U.S. and Europe. Graveyard imagery, such as this skull with crossbones, gave way to gentler images of death. (See pages 56-58.) | Today our burials are as varied as in the past, and they change rapidly, too. In Ghana, the Ga people bury their dead in colorful coffins, such as this one shaped as a leopard and made for a hunter. |

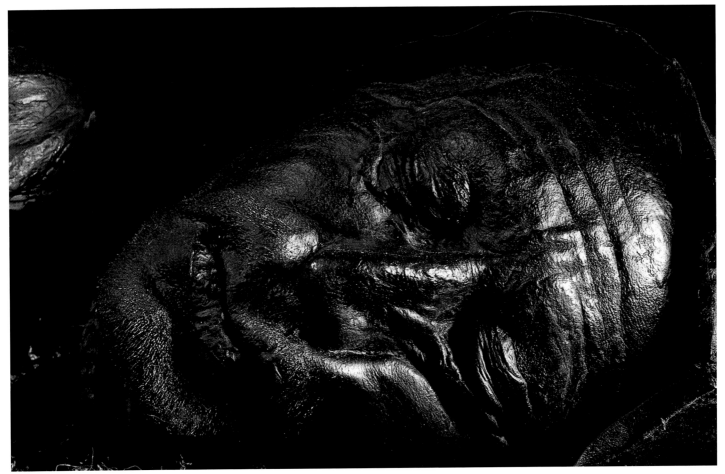

Among the world's best preserved bodies from the past are the "bog people" from northern Europe and the British Isles. They were accidentally preserved in swamps where their bodies were placed between 1000 B.C. and A.D. 200. The acidic conditions turned the skin of this man, found in 1952 in Tollund, Denmark, into leather.

Egypt Prepares for the Afterlife

The 3,200-year-old mummified remains of the pharaoh Ramses II show successful preservation of a corpse. The Egyptians believed that if the soul could not find the body after death, it would become lost.

The most famous mummies are those of the ancient Egyptians. They are the most numerous, too, with an estimated count in the millions. We know how the Egyptians made mummies from reading the writings of ancient priests and from studying the bodies themselves. After washing a corpse, priests took the heart, liver, intestines, and other internal organs out of the body and set them aside in jars. Then they sewed the body up and placed it in a salt called natron to dry it out. When the corpse was dry, they wrapped it tightly in long strips of cloth, then placed it in a coffin called a sarcophagus.

How and why Egyptians began their unique burial customs remains a mystery. Perhaps early Egyptians noticed how corpses dried out when left in the hot and sandy Nile Valley. Early burials of such dry bodies, including ones wrapped in linen and resin, show that Egyptians may have experimented with different methods of preservation until about 2600 B.C.—the dawn of the age of pyramid building. By that time Egyptians had a strong belief in the afterlife. They thought that as long as the body was preserved, the soul could find the body and participate in life after death. This is why mummification became such a desirable part of their funeral ritual.

Other cultures who lived near Egypt in ancient times also believed in immortality and practiced body preservation. The Babylonians, Persians, and Syrians all experimented with it by covering corpses in honey or wax to prevent decay caused by bacteria. Alexander the Great, the Greek who conquered Egypt and much of western Asia about 300 B.C., died in Babylon and is said to have been preserved this way. The Egyptians, however, practiced mummification as part of their funerary rituals longer

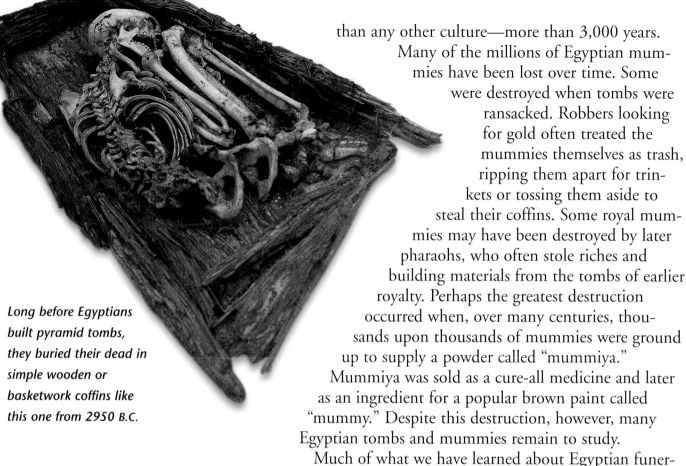

Long before Egyptians built pyramid tombs, they buried their dead in simple wooden or basketwork coffins like this one from 2950 B.C.

than any other culture—more than 3,000 years. Many of the millions of Egyptian mummies have been lost over time. Some were destroyed when tombs were ransacked. Robbers looking for gold often treated the mummies themselves as trash, ripping them apart for trinkets or tossing them aside to steal their coffins. Some royal mummies may have been destroyed by later pharaohs, who often stole riches and building materials from the tombs of earlier royalty. Perhaps the greatest destruction occurred when, over many centuries, thousands upon thousands of mummies were ground up to supply a powder called "mummiya." Mummiya was sold as a cure-all medicine and later as an ingredient for a popular brown paint called "mummy." Despite this destruction, however, many Egyptian tombs and mummies remain to study.

Much of what we have learned about Egyptian funerary rituals comes from papyrus texts buried in some tombs along with mummies. These writings made up a religious work called the Book of the Dead. The Book of the Dead was meant to serve as a guide for those who passed away and to provide them with assistance on their journey into the next life. The book describes a passage through an underground world ruled by the god-king, Osiris.

To prepare the deceased for this underworld, the Book of the Dead describes an "opening of the mouth" ritual to be performed on a newly mummified corpse. The Egyptians believed this gave the dead person a magical new breath of life before he or she went on to face many tests and obstacles, including a final judgment by Osiris. The Book of the Dead would help the dead pass through these tests and continue on to enjoy the pleasures of the afterlife they had planned for. Any worldly wealth placed in tombs would be available in the afterlife, and objects illustrated on tomb walls would be there as well. The more belongings an Egyptian could afford to have placed in his tomb or painted on its walls, the better off he would be in his next life.

From the time of the earliest pharaohs, preparing for the afterlife was one of the most important things a ruler could do. These first kings were buried in large tombs called mastabas, low brick buildings built over burial chambers dug into the ground. A large group of such tombs was built at Abydos, a sacred city far up the Nile where, according to the myths, Osiris himself was buried. Some powerful Egyptians who were planning to be buried somewhere else also built secondary empty tombs, or cenotaphs, at Abydos just to have a tomb near Osiris. The large number of mastabas made the funeral grounds at Abydos look like a city. It and other tomb complexes

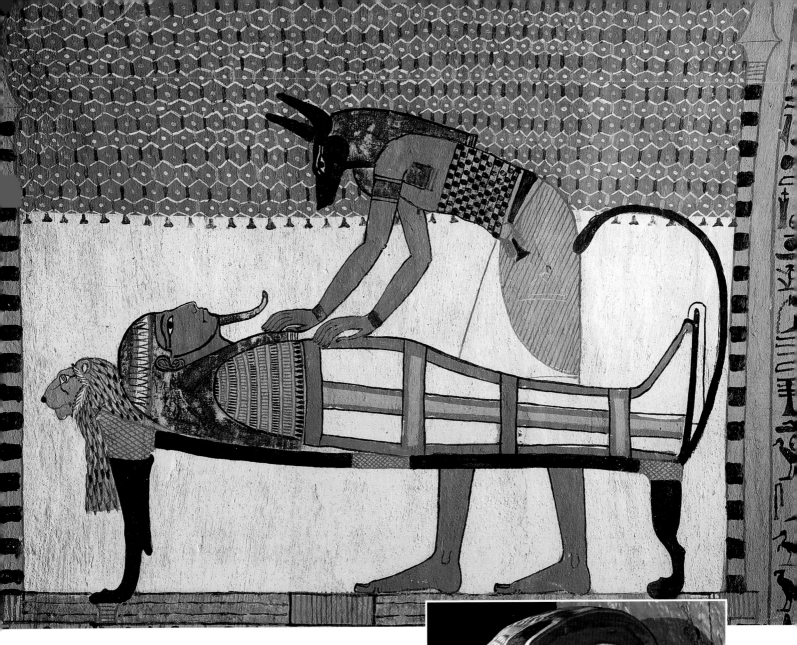

How to Make a Mummy

Over thousands of years the Egyptians became masters of the craft of preserving corpses. After removing several organs and the brain from a body, they used herbs that killed bacteria to sterilize it. The body was then dried, wrapped in many layers of linen strips, and placed in a sarcophagus.

When the mummy was ready to be put into a tomb, the priests put on masks to appear like the jackal-headed god of mummification, Anubis (above). They then conducted ceremonies to prepare the deceased for life after death.

High technology such as CT scans allows us to learn more about mummification without unwrapping mummies. At right, the scan of a mummy with a painted linen face from 300 B.C. shows its many inner layers and the skeleton inside.

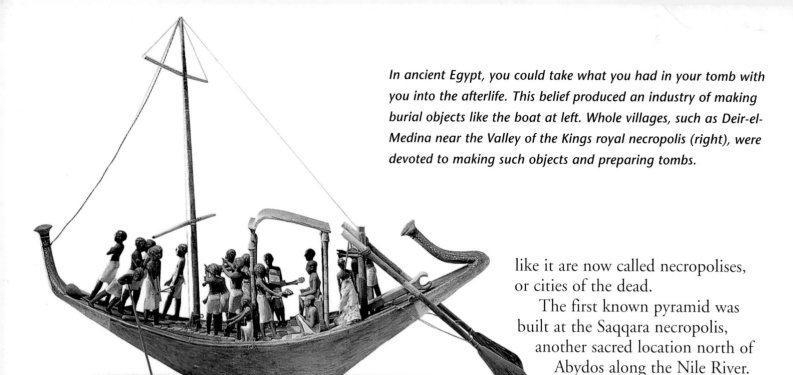

In ancient Egypt, you could take what you had in your tomb with you into the afterlife. This belief produced an industry of making burial objects like the boat at left. Whole villages, such as Deir-el-Medina near the Valley of the Kings royal necropolis (right), were devoted to making such objects and preparing tombs.

like it are now called necropolises, or cities of the dead.

The first known pyramid was built at the Saqqara necropolis, another sacred location north of Abydos along the Nile River. The Egyptian architect Imhotep is said to have built the pyramid for the pharaoh Zoser and his family. It started out as a mastaba and was later added to in stages until it looked something like a wedding cake. This is why it is known as the Step Pyramid. Under this pyramid is a maze of vertical shafts and tunnels leading to deep chambers once filled with grave goods. Surrounding the pyramid is a high wall. Inside the wall are many buildings built especially for the pharaoh's comfort in the afterlife.

Pharaohs after Zoser experimented with pyramids of their own. One pharaoh named Snefru built three. His first pyramid, the Meidum Pyramid, was a step pyramid. His second project, the Bent Pyramid, is the first known attempt to build a true pyramid. Construction started at a steep angle of 55 degrees at the bottom, and then halfway up the angle was changed to a more gentle slope of 43.5 degrees. His third pyramid, the Northern Stone Pyramid, was the first successful true pyramid. Snefru's son, grandson, and great grandson built the best known of the pyramids—the three great pyramids at Giza. For 4,500 years these tombs have amazed all who have seen them. They are one of the seven wonders of the ancient world.

Evolution of the Pyramid Tomb

The earliest known pyramid is the Step Pyramid of Zoser. After this came Snefru's step pyramid at Meidum, which had smooth sides built over it later. Eventually Egyptians built structures on the scale of the Great Pyramid of Khufu at Giza. By the time of Pepi II, the last pyramid builder, the size of pyramids had shrunk considerably.

Step Pyramid of Zoser at Saqqara 2630 B.C.

Pyramid of Snefru at Meidum 2600 B.C.

Bent Pyramid of Snefru at Dashur 2600 B.C.

Northern Stone Pyramid of Snefru at Dashur 2600 B.C.

Great Pyramid of Khufu at Giza 2520 B.C.

Pepi II's pyramid at Saqqara 2250 B.C.

With their small tombs (above) the pyramid builders attempted to capture some of the grandeur of royal tombs. Egyptian traditions were so strong that long after the pyramid-building era, after Greeks and then Romans had conquered the area, they still influenced burial practices. A mummy from 322 B.C. (left) reflects two cultures. It is an Egyptian-style mummy buried with a coin (inset) to pay the ferryman for a ride across the Styx River to the underworld of the Greeks.

Though archaeologists have been studying Egyptian tombs for more than a hundred years, these monuments to the rulers of ancient Egypt still present mysteries. One of these mysteries is, "How did Egyptians organize their society to build the pyramids?" Today, Dr. Mark Lehner and Dr. Zahi Hawass are studying the Giza pyramids and the surrounding area in great detail to find the answer. Dr. Lehner's excavations show that near the pyramids are houses, bakeries, and workshops where people lived and prepared food and tools for thousands of workers and managers involved in pyramid construction.

Dr. Hawass discovered the cemetery of these pyramid builders on a nearby hill. Most workers were buried in modest graves without mummification. Some of the bodies buried there show that pyramid building was not an easy life. Broken arm and leg bones appear frequently among the workers. Higher on the hillside, some higher-ranking pyramid builders, with titles such as "overseer of masonry," and "inspector of the craftsmen," managed to build small tombs. Some of them have miniature pyramids on top. Inscriptions on tomb doors and walls prepared them for the afterlife, just like the much larger tombs of royalty. Not only were these Egyptians preparing a glorious afterlife for their pharaohs, they were claiming a little bit of it for themselves.

Golden Tombs of the Amazons

The golden costume of a Scythian noblewoman surrounds her bones as they were found deep in a tomb in Ukraine. Women of the Scytho-Siberian culture were powerful and had a reputation for being fearsome warriors. Near the spot where her heart once was lies a bronze mirror.

Arctic Ocean

UKRAINE
GREECE   ★Moscow
RUSSIA   Siberia
Black
Sea   Pazyryk burials

Herodotus was a fifth-century Greek historian who stirred the world's imagination with stories of the Scythians, barbaric nomads who lived near the Black Sea. According to his stories they performed human sacrifices, ate human flesh, and drank from cups made from the skulls of their enemies. He called their women Amazons and said they were fierce ax-wielding horsewomen who fought as equals alongside men. Herodotus's stories made fascinating reading, but were they true?

In the early part of the 20th century, archaeologists interested in this question began excavating Scythian burial mounds, called kurgans, located in Ukraine by the Black Sea. There they discovered that Herodotus was only partly right. Yes, the Scythians had a warlike side. Cups made from skulls, scalped corpses, and many axes and arrows were found in their graves. Many Scythian females were found buried with weapons, too, supporting Herodotus's description of them as Amazons. Yet, there was another side to Scythian culture that Herodotus did not write about. Archaeologists learned that the Scythians loved horses, beautiful golden objects, and elaborate clothing and tattoos. They probably spent most of their time tending their flocks, not killing their neighbors. They were one of many groups of semi-nomadic herdsmen called the Scytho-Siberians who roamed over thousands of miles of steppe, grassland that stretches from the Black Sea all the way to eastern Siberia. Their culture lasted from about 800 B.C. to 100 B.C.

Scytho-Siberian burials suggest that in addition to being warriors, women enjoyed a social prestige and responsibility far beyond that known by women of other cultures of that time. They shared life with men—and that means not only the

Scytho-Siberian tombs are known not only for their gold, but for their fine objects made from felt and wood. This is a Pazyryk saddle cover made from felt, leather, and horsehair from a fifth-century B.C. burial. Its decoration shows a mythical griffin with an ibex's horns in its beak.

time-consuming tasks of tending of herds, caring for homes, and moving from place to place, but hunting and fighting as well.

The Scytho-Siberian culture was a loose-knit group that included the Scythians in the west, the people of Pazyryk in the east, and many other groups in between. Because of the great distance between the Scythians and Pazyryks—similar to the distance between Los Angeles and New York City—it is unlikely that these two groups of people ever actually saw each other. Yet it is clear that they were in contact through trade. Excavations of a burial containing a young woman in southern Russia, for example, revealed a bronze mirror from faraway China along with her golden necklaces, bracelets, and battle-ax. Scytho-Siberians traded horses, meat, furs, wool, wheat, and fish for the wine, oil, and gold jewelry available from Greek city dwellers in the west.

Some Scytho-Siberian tombs contained great hoards of golden objects. Although the precious metal is valuable, the illustrations carved on the objects make them priceless to archaeologists.

They show the Scythians hunting, fighting, and also tending to their horses and other livestock. In tombs discovered in Central Asia and Siberia, archaeologists have found beautiful objects made of wood and felt depicting both real and imaginary animals. They suggest that the lives of these nomads were intertwined with their animals and the natural world. Much of what we know of the appearance and lifestyle of the Scytho-Siberians we've learned from studying these images from the tombs.

Each Scytho-Siberian tomb has a shaft in its center, which extends to a wooden room built deep in the earth. The Scytho-Siberians built these rooms with special care. The outer surface of the room was left rough, but the inside was finished as if it were a cabin. Within the chamber, the deceased were placed in log coffins, with heads facing to the east. Clothing, weapons, tools, food, and jewelry were placed about the tomb or inside the coffin. The Scytho-Siberians' most prized possessions, their horses, were sacrificed and placed just outside the room. It is as if the tomb chamber were a home with horses waiting outside to take the dead to another world. Perhaps the construction of homelike tombs is a reflection of a strong Scytho-Siberian connection to family and their nomadic homes.

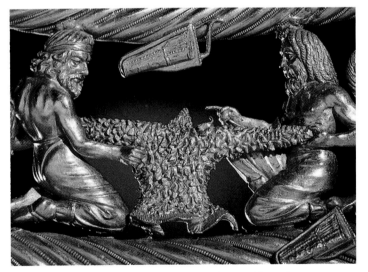 

A burial mound in Ukraine yielded this golden chest ornament called a pectoral (above). It is 12 inches across and weighs 3.3 pounds. Delicately shaped figures on the object show scenes of the daily life of Scythians. Among the scenes are two men with a sheepskin, with quivers for their arrows nearby (left, close-up), and a boy milking a sheep (right, close-up).

Displays of gold may have been part of Scythian funeral processions, such as the one imagined here. According to Herodotus, the Scythians tore out their hair and cut themselves to show their grief as the remains of chiefs passed by.

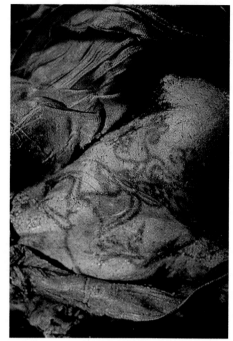

A burial mound in the grassy steppes of Siberia (opposite page) held a treasure more valuable than gold. It was a burial frozen in time. It took three days for archaeologists to remove the corpse of a Pazyryk woman from a block of ice that lay in an eight-foot-long log coffin within the tomb (above, left). When the ice thawed, an elaborate head-dress and a costume of silk and wool were revealed. Her tattooed shoulder (above, right) displayed a creature (right) similar to ones seen in Scytho-Siberian artifacts.

Often more than one person was buried in a kurgan. Since it is unlikely that two related people would have died at the same time, archaeologists think that the extra people may be relatives who were buried later in the same tomb. In a very few cases the arrangement of bodies and condition of bones found in graves suggests that other people may have been sacrificed to join a relative or master in death. Despite Herodotus's tales, however, human sacrifice seems to have been the exception, not the rule.

In 1993, Dr. Natalia Polosmak discovered a remarkably preserved kurgan in the remote Ukok plateau of Siberia. Just 10 yards from a fence guarding the Russian-Chinese border, she dug into a small tomb. After spending two weeks removing tons of stones, she found the bodies of a man and three horses. His tomb had been looted, but on a hunch that this man's burial was not the first on this site, she kept on digging. It was not long before she hit the roof of a timber burial chamber. It was an undisturbed Pazyryk burial.

The tomb was deep enough to penetrate the permafrost, a layer of permanently frozen earth that lies beneath the Siberian plains. This natural refrigeration caused the burial contents to be well preserved. Inside the chamber, as if they had been left there yesterday, were a coffin and a small table with a food offering of mutton. There was even a knife sticking in the mutton. The bodies of six horses lying outside the chamber still had their coats of hair. Such a well-preserved Scytho-Siberian tomb had not been found for more than 40 years.

Dr. Polosmak focused on the log coffin. On opening it, she discovered a solid block of ice. Hundreds of years before, water had seeped into the coffin and frozen. Not knowing whether there was anything in the ice or not, she began a three-day process of melting it. The archaeologist's patience paid off. The melted ice revealed the preserved body of a young woman who died 2,500 years ago. She became known as the "Ice Maiden."

The Ice Maiden's body had been prepared for preservation by removing her brain, eyes, and vital organs. In their places were herbs and grasses and even balls of fur for her eye sockets. Herodotus had told how Scythian chieftains were similarly preserved and then displayed for weeks before being buried in a mound. The Ice Maiden must have been important as well.

Though the fur cloak that once covered her body had decayed, the Ice Maiden's Chinese silk blouse, woolen skirt, and other clothing, including a three-foot-tall headdress, were perfectly preserved. Also preserved were her elaborate tattoos of animals.

Further studies of the Ice Maiden, including DNA tests, will tell us more about her Pazyryk culture. It may be that she is related to people who still inhabit that area. Their horse-riding skills and other customs echo those of the Scytho-Siberian culture of long ago.

Ghost Soldiers of the Emperor

A clay soldier stands only partially free of dirt in a trench where he and thousands like him guard the tomb of Qin Shi Huang Di, an emperor who ruled China 2,200 years ago. Craftsmen used molds of different kinds of soldiers to mass-produce the figures. Archers, foot soldiers, and generals each have uniforms, weapons, and hairstyles that reflect their rank and duties.

Deep within a man-made mountain in northern China lies the body of Qin Shi Huang Di, the first emperor of a unified China. After 2,200 years, his burial chamber near the city of Xi'an is still unexcavated, but archaeologists have been working for more than 20 years excavating the enormous tomb complex, which is the size of a small city. The complex includes the central tomb mound, a palace, and courtyards. Its most amazing feature is the thousands of life-size clay statues of warriors and horse-drawn chariots that lie in football field-size pits to the east of the emperor. They stand at attention in neat ranks that seem ready for inspection or a march to war. It took 700,000 people 36 years to build this tomb complex, the grandest of any ever excavated in China.

Along the Yellow River at Anyang are the large tombs of other emperors. These, however, are from the Shang dynasty, one thousand years earlier than Qin Shi Huang Di, a time when a powerful clan ruled a part of China. There is one important difference between their graves and that of the Qin emperor. The figures surrounding the Shang royalty are not clay models. They are the remains of real people and animals sacrificed as part of the imperial burial ritual. Decapitated adult males found lying in rows around Shang tombs may have been prisoners of war, but human sacrifices inside the tomb included imperial family members and servants. One burial contained more than 165 human sacrifices.

Qin Shi Huang Di was a military leader who proclaimed himself the first emperor of the Qin dynasty after conquering a group of squabbling states and forming the country of China. He ordered standardized systems of writing, currency, weights, and measures. He even standardized the axle width of wagons

A Qin soldier watches prisoners carry freshly painted clay soldiers to their places in pits that surround the emperor's tomb during a minister's surprise inspection (left). The soldier is holding a halberd and is dressed in armor similar to suits of stone found at the site (above).

and chariots to make sure all the grooves worn in roads were consistent, making them much easier to travel.

The Qin emperor may have been a wise leader in some ways, but he was far from kind. He buried alive scholars he disagreed with and used forced labor in the building of the 3,000-mile-long Great Wall of China. Though he spared the lives of soldiers and horses by substituting clay models for his tomb, ancient Chinese records say

Rebellious peasants armed with torches storm through a doorway in this depiction of their effort to destroy the tomb of Qin Shi Huang Di. Many parts of the tomb complex were destroyed in their attack, including much of the clay army (right). Whether or not the elaborate inner tomb shown above was damaged remains to be discovered.

that other victims lie there. Members of the imperial family, as well as the artisans and craftsmen who built the tomb, followed him to his grave.

Old written records also tell of the magnificence of Qin Shi Huang Di's as yet unopened tomb chamber. The ceiling of the room is said to be a map of the heavens floating above his coffin. The floor is described as a huge map of the empire with liquid mercury flowing in channels to mark China's rivers and lakes.

The Qin dynasty lasted only three years after the emperor's death in 210 B.C. His son was assassinated soon afterward in a rebellion spawned by hatred of the emperor. During the revolt, peasants broke into the emperor's tomb, smashed much of the clay army, and set fire to the timber structure. This rebellion led to the establishment of the Han dynasty, which ruled China for the next 400 years.

Han emperors followed the example set by Qin Shi Huang Di and built massive tomb complexes filled with clay soldiers. Yet unlike the first clay army, the army buried with the fourth Han emperor, Han Jing Di, was created in miniature. This is probably an early reflection of the

Provisions for the miniature army of Han emperor Jing Di included rows of clay sheep and pigs placed several layers deep in trenches that surround the central tomb (left). Each clay soldier (above) was painted, clothed in fabric, and then supplied with weapons (right) before being placed in rows.

traditional Chinese belief that the world of the afterlife is a miniature version of this world. According to this view, souls are smaller versions of their owners.

From the times of the early Chinese dynasties such as the Shang, Qin, and Han, those who buried the dead were trying to create a home for them in the afterlife that mirrored the world of the living. So aside from their armies, royalty were also buried with figures of acrobats and dancers, servants, bronze pots, food, and jade jewelry. By studying how the Chinese of different times built tombs and what they placed within them, we can see not only what ancient China looked like but how they thought about death as well.

Echoes of the past can still be found in Chinese burial practices today. Funerals are often accompanied by the burning of paper models of houses, cars, TVs, credit cards, and even cans of beer. Paper money, called "hell money," is burnt as well. The hope is that these offerings will make the dead more comfortable in the afterlife and prevent them from returning to haunt the living as demanding spirits called "hungry ghosts." Today, the annual Hungry Ghost festival is an opportunity for relatives to repeat offerings to ancestors to keep them happy. It is part of a tradition that has persisted in one form or another in China for more than 4,000 years.

47

Tombs of the Moche Lords

This gold-and-copper burial mask once covered the face of a Moche lord buried at Dos Cabezas more than 1,500 years ago. Moche finds such as this are rare due to centuries of grave robbing in the area.

PERU

Sipán
Dos Cabezas
Lima ★
Pacific Ocean

The large mud-brick tombs built by the Moche people loom over the coastal desert of Peru. Between A.D. 200 and A.D. 800, the Moche irrigated the area with a network of diverted rivers and canals, turning the desert into gardens of corn, beans, potatoes, and squash. Now, almost 2,000 years later, the Moche and their irrigation system are long gone. The place is one of the driest deserts on Earth, and the tomb pyramids of Moche nobility are just dusty mounds of dirt.

Centuries of grave robbing have left the Moche's once-stately pyramids pockmarked with pits. The thieving started when Europeans arrived in the 16th century and continues to this day, with robbers selling stolen artifacts on the international art market or to tourists.

In 1987 grave robbers digging near Sipán, Peru, found the motherlode. It was a Moche royal tomb filled with precious metals, ceramics, and textiles. Somehow this final resting place of a Moche lord had remained undiscovered for more than 1,500 years.

A few days after the discovery, a squabble over how to divide the booty broke out among the robbers. One of them was upset with the others and reported the find to local authorities. When police raided the homes of the looters, they discovered some of the precious items. Immediately the police called in archaeologists, who in turn sealed off the site and protected it with round-the-clock armed guards. The scientists then began a years-long excavation of what turned out to be several Moche burials in one tomb.

Over the course of the dig, the richness of the Moche culture became clear, as did the power and wealth of the rulers. The

In the plains of Peru, eroding tomb mounds are all that remain of the ancient civilizations that once lived there. In the area in the left foreground of the photograph, grave robbers dug 23 feet deep and discovered a rich royal burial. Unfortunately, they destroyed archaeological evidence, including buried bodies, in the process.

burials, which range in date from about A.D. 200 to A.D. 500, contained many layers of well-crafted ceramics, beautiful textiles, and objects of gold, silver, and copper. The tomb also held sacrificial victims, some of whose feet had been cut off.

One of the first burials encountered in the upper layers of the tomb was a large wooden box containing a male dressed in an amazing costume. Two of the archaeologists working there, Dr. Walter Alva and Dr. Christopher Donnan, noticed that this costumed figure was eerily similar in appearance to a warrior priest commonly seen in Moche ceramics. The ceramics often show the priest with a dog at his feet. He wears a large headdress decorated with a big crescent-shaped ornament and is surrounded by others who present him with prisoners. The prisoners are shown tied up and stripped of clothing and weapons. It appears they are to be sacrificed and that their blood will soon fill the cup being offered to the warrior priest.

The buried man—who has become known as the Lord of Sipán—wore the same headdress as the priest who appears on the ceramics. He was surrounded with other symbols of war and power, such as ceremonial battle clubs and golden rattles decorated with scenes of human sacrifice. He was also surrounded by five other human bodies and a dog. Could he have been a warrior priest like those shown on the pots? Dr. Donnan thinks so. He suggests that the roles of the characters illustrated on the pots were played in real life by Moche leaders.

At the time of its discovery, the Lord of Sipán's grave was the richest Moche burial ever found.

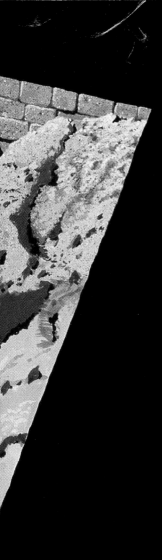

Inside the Burial of a Moche Lord

About 1,500 years ago the Moche prepared one of the most elaborate burials ever discovered in the Western Hemisphere —the grave for a ruler archaeologists call the Lord of Sipán (left). He was buried along with five other people. Twelve feet down, and above logs forming the roof of his tomb, was the body of a young man with a copper helmet and shield who seems to guard the burial. Young women were buried at the Lord of Sipán's head and feet. At his sides were men in their 40s, one of whom was buried with a dog. For some reason the young guard and the women were missing feet.

The Lord of Sipán himself was buried in the center in a large wooden coffin with copper strapping. Inside was an amazing array of ceremonial objects and burial wrappings that surrounded him and his costume (right).

These included feathers for a headdress (a), and many pieces of gold, silver, and copper jewelry (b). Some of this jewelry was in the style of the warrior priest figure, such as the golden nose-piece and crescent-shaped headdress (c). In his hands he held ingots of gold and copper as well as a rattle and a knife. On his back were gold and copper backflaps (d). Oyster shells (e), which were valuable and had religious meaning for many American cultures, appear in several different areas of the coffin.

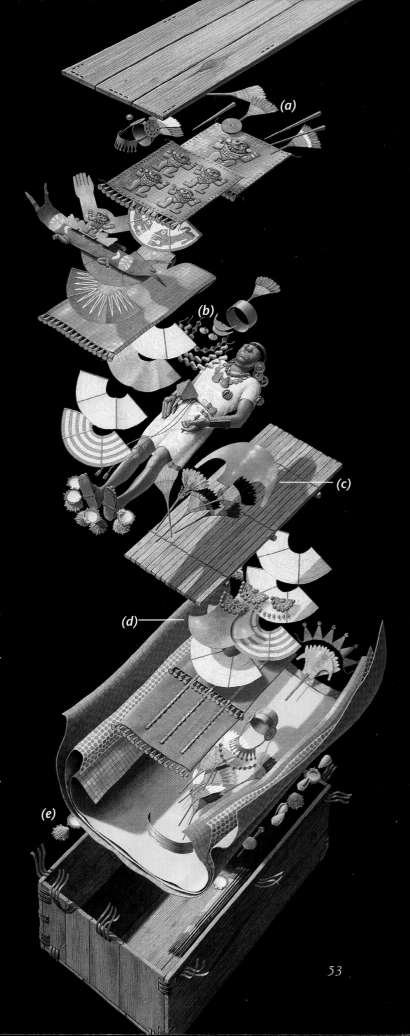

(a)

(b)

(c)

(d)

(e)

The bones of a Moche nobleman buried at Dos Cabezas lie by the side of a young woman who was probably sacrificed as part of a funerary ritual (above). These burials were discovered undisturbed by archaeologist Dr. Christopher Donnan, who is shown here sifting through grave goods with a colleague. Among the objects found were the tarnished remains of an elaborate golden headdress (below, left) and a nose-piece shaped like a bat—a symbol of human sacrifice (below, right).

A few years later, however, when Dr. Alva dug deeper into the tomb mound at Sipán, he was astonished to find an equally spectacular grave from the earliest days of the Moche, about A.D. 200. Again a central male figure was surrounded by grave goods and other bodies. Alva dubbed the new find the "Old Lord of Sipán." From this one mound, archaeologists were able to study hundreds of years of Moche culture.

Even more recently, Dr. Donnan discovered another set of early Moche burials south of Sipán. These graves, which he dated to about A.D. 500, were found in a huge mound of mud brick called Dos Cabezas, or "two heads." It got this name because someone looking for treasure had long ago dug a trench through the middle of what was once a pyramid, creating two smaller mounds that stand side by side like two heads.

Wearing a bat-shaped nose-piece and golden headdress, the Moche nobleman buried at Dos Cabezas may have looked something like this. We don't know if he ever used these burial items, or his shield and club, in life.

The graves Dr. Donnan discovered within Dos Cabezas were lined up in a row and contained the remains of three men. The bodies of several young women, maybe victims of human sacrifice, were placed nearby, along with llamas and pottery. Miniature burials were discovered near each grave. Copper dolls and other artifacts in these mini-graves suggest that they were copies of the contents of the real burials.

The three males buried at Dos Cabezas, though, were anything but small. The average Moche male grew to between four feet ten inches and five feet six inches in height. The men buried in the main graves at Dos Cabezas were five feet nine inches to six feet tall—true giants for their time. Further study of the skeletons will tell archaeologists more about these important people, including whether or not their size was the result of a genetic disorder. Perhaps their size set them apart from others in their time.

The real value of unlooted tombs like those of Sipán and Dos Cabezas is not the gold and jewelry, but the opportunity to study burials just as they were left hundreds of years ago. The arrangement of the graves and grave goods surrounding both Lords of Sipán and those buried at Dos Cabezas are important to understanding the relationships of the individuals and their symbolic roles. If these graves had been looted by grave robbers, the chance to understand them would have been lost forever.

Reading Our Own Remains

The Day of the Dead is celebrated in Mexico with candy skulls and gaily colored paper skeletons (left). On that day, people flock to the cemeteries to visit the graves of their ancestors. This funerary ritual would leave very few remains for future archaeologists. On the other hand, cemetery statues such as this mourning maiden (below) could last for centuries.

The discovery of a burial from a long-lost culture can show a lot about how those people lived. Each discovered burial is like a snapshot of a particular place at a specific moment in time. But interpreting finds is not easy. We do not know what long-gone people were thinking when they buried their dead. By studying the remains—or lack of remains—of our own burial rituals, scientists can improve their understanding of the past.

Many modern rituals leave remains that may endure for centuries. Among these are cemeteries with stone gravestones and tombs, burial mounds built with rocks, coffins built of hardwood, metals, and fiberglass, and millions of urns containing the ashes of the cremated.

These modern remains are already being studied by archaeologists. Dr. Sarah Tarlow discovered an unexpected story while studying cemeteries in North America and Europe. She learned how quickly people can change the way they think about death.

Dr. Tarlow noticed that many more tombstones were made in the 1800s than in the 1700s and that the designs and inscriptions on the stones had changed dramatically as well. Skulls and crossbones on tombstones in the 1700s had given way to other, more gentle symbols in the next century. Statues of angels and cherubs as well as images of weeping willows began to appear. Simple initials for names gave way not just to the full names of loved ones, but to tender inscriptions or poems.

Dr. Tarlow thinks this had to do with a change in the quality of life. People in the 1800s had more money and better sanitation and medicine than those of the 1700s. This resulted in longer lives, loving marriages and families, and an atmosphere where people could express their emotions more freely. A part of

Rebury or Study?

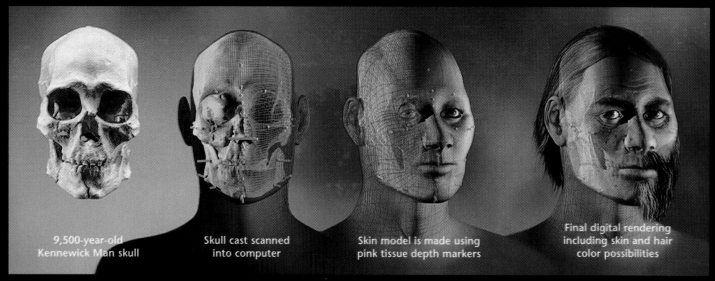

9,500-year-old Kennewick Man skull | Skull cast scanned into computer | Skin model is made using pink tissue depth markers | Final digital rendering including skin and hair color possibilities

Native American burial grounds are considered sacred. As a result, some native groups are offended when graves of their ancestors are disturbed. They see little difference between the activities of tomb looters and those of archaeologists. When the 9,500-year-old bones of a man were found near Kennewick, Washington, Native American groups and scientists showed equal interest in obtaining the remains. A step-by-step reconstruction of the Kennewick Man skull shows what he may have looked like in life (above).

In the United States and Australia, native groups have brought attention to long histories of disrespect for their burial grounds. As a result, new laws have been passed requiring museums and universities to return bones and grave goods they have collected over the years. These remains are then reclaimed and buried.

Some archaeologists fear that valuable information is lost when remains are reburied before they have been studied and when excavations of ancient sites are prohibited. One solution that shows promise is increased collaboration between archaeologists and native groups. This can result in finding ways to study burials while still showing respect for the dead.

this greater freedom of emotion was that people felt they could publicly show their feelings of loss when a loved one died. Many people saw tombstones as a way of making their grief public and marking a spot where they could visit the deceased. These changes took place within 200 years—a blink of an eye in archaeological time. Now, looking at remains from the more distant past, archaeologists know that changes in symbols or designs can mean many things that are not obvious, and can occur over very short periods of time.

Another thing archaeologists can see by studying recent burial rituals is that they can be dramatically affected by technology. The invention of modern embalming during the American Civil War, for example, changed the pattern of American funerals in only 50 years.

Before the war, most Americans were placed in wooden coffins and buried as quickly as possible after they died. Ice was the only thing available to delay the rotting of a corpse if a funeral could not take place immediately. So people were generally buried close to where they died.

Families of war dead during the Civil War therefore had a problem. How could they get their dead back from faraway battlefields before they decomposed? President Abraham Lincoln addressed this problem by ordering a new method of embalming service be provided to families. It was developed by a military doctor and involved replacing the fluids in corpses with a chemical preservative. This preserved their bodies long enough to get them home. A short time after the war, Lincoln was assassinated. His body was embalmed using this new technology and taken home to Illinois to be buried almost a month after his death.

By the early 20th century, embalming had become popular in the United States, and it was common for bodies to travel long distances for burial. Someone who had left his hometown as a child could return to be buried as if he had never left. So now the location of a grave in the United States may tell us nothing about where the person died.

The impact of modern embalming in other countries was quite different from its impact in the United States. Many countries reserve embalming for important people whose bodies will be on long public display. In China, for example, more than 100 million people have filed past the embalmed body of the first leader of the People's Republic of China, Chairman Mao Zedong, since he died in 1976. In other countries, such as Denmark, embalming is against the law. This is because Denmark is a small country short on cemetery space. Artificially preserving bodies there would only make their problem worse.

Looking back at ancient graveyards, archaeologists are careful not to assume anything. As the example in the United States shows, a new burial method can suddenly change both when and where people are buried. Today's archaeologists also know that different cultures of the past may have used the same technology in different ways.

Another practice that can blur the archaeological picture is the moving and reburial of bones. Once bones are removed from their original resting place, the story of each burial becomes more difficult to figure out. In recent times, reburials have occurred when old cemeteries needed to be moved to make room for construction. Skeletons in museum collections also are being reburied today. Among these are the remains of Native Americans and Australian aborigines that were collected by archaeologists many years ago.

Burial practices around the world today are highly varied, and each has significance that is hard to understand without more information than the burials themselves provide. From top to bottom: The Tomb of the Unknown Soldier in Arlington, Virginia; a cremation ceremony in India by the Ganges River; and an ecological burial near London.

Today in Ghana, the Ga people bury their dead in coffins made in the shape of cars, fish, and other animals (above), and the Dani people of Irian Jaya (opposite) preserve their great warriors by smoking them. They believe this will preserve their fighting spirit.

Over the centuries, bones lying in overcrowded cemeteries have been moved to new sites or to storage areas called charnel houses or ossuaries. One unusual ossuary in a church near Prague, Czech Republic, has thousands of bones from its old cemetery hung up on its walls in decorative patterns. In 19th-century Paris, cemeteries became so overcrowded that millions of bones had to be moved to underground tunnels outside of town.

A study of reburied European royalty who died away from home between A.D. 1000 and A.D. 1500 led to a new interpretation of some ancient burials. Because they were important people, and because they lived in a place and time when people kept written records, good historical records were kept of what happened to them. Their bodies were reduced to bone by being cut into pieces and boiled in wine, vinegar, or water. This allowed the bones to be transported long distances. Many skeletons treated and transported this way lost parts in the process. Estella Weiss-Krejci, an archaeologist who studies Maya burials in Mexico and Central America, recognized that the bones left in Maya tombs showed a pattern of missing bones similar to that of the reburied European royalty. Earlier archaeologists had explained the bones as evidence the Maya took bodies apart during ritual human sacrifice. Dr. Weiss-Krejci suggests that the Maya may simply have been moving and reburying their dead nobility just as the Europeans did. This interpretation could apply to bone collections of other ancient cultures as well.

Although moving bones makes interpretation harder, burials that leave no remains make it impossible. Partly because cemeteries are getting crowded, many people in North America and Europe today are practicing nontraditional ways of burying the dead that leave no trace at all. In an ecological, or green, burial, for example, the deceased may be buried in a cardboard coffin and the gravesite marked with a wooden plaque or living trees and bushes. It is also popular today to spread the ashes of a cremated loved one at a favorite place, such as a good fishing hole or a hiking path. Some people hire a plane to spread ashes over a wide area of land or sea. Some families mix ashes of a loved one into a cement block to be dropped into the ocean, to become part of an artificial reef. Others float the deceased into the sky on high-altitude balloons or pack them into fireworks for an explosive send-off. The ashes of Gene Rodenberry, the creator of the popular TV show *Star Trek*, were shot into space on a private rocket.

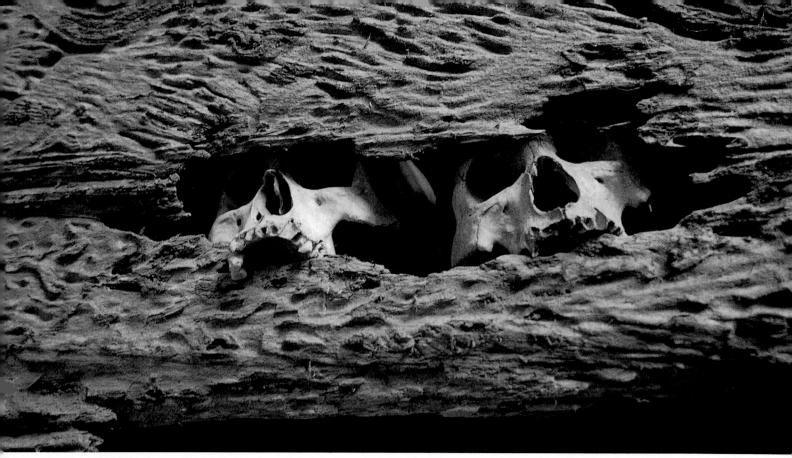

Two skulls peer out from within an erong, a beautifully carved wooden coffin that serves as an ossuary for the ancestors of the Torajan people who live on the island of Sulawesi in Indonesia.

Yet burials that leave no trace are nothing new. Many traditional rituals leave little or no remains. Jewish people, for example, bury their dead in soft pine coffins to promote decay. Hindus cremate their dead, then pour the ashes into the Ganges River. Tibetans neither bury nor cremate, but cut up their dead, mix them with flour, and feed them to the birds in what is called a sky burial.

How many burials like these are we missing when we look back in time? We may never know, but we do know that many ancient peoples, such as those living in the British Isles during the Bronze Age (2750 B.C. to 700 B.C.), practiced cremation and left few burial remains. Fortunately, we can learn about some of these cultures from other evidence, such as the ruins of villages and forts they left behind. It is quite possible, however, that some cultures left no trace at all.

When we look back at ancient burials, it is important to keep our own burial practices in view. The variety of customs today is probably a good measure of what was going on in the past. It is important to look at all of the possible interpretations of how an ancient people lived instead of concluding that the physical remains give us the whole story.

We can also look at our own burial practices not just to learn about the past, but to learn about the present. From changing tombstone designs to launching ashes into space, funerary rituals reflect what people are thinking about life and death. The materials and rituals we use in burials reflect our technologies and economic conditions and where we are from. People of the future will probably see the remains of some of our burial practices and be as fascinated by them as we are by those of civilizations who lived before us. Will they be able to guess correctly what we were thinking when we buried the dead?

Bibliography

O ne of the pleasures of working at NATIONAL GEOGRAPHIC magazine is that every day brings something new. In my 10 years of directing artwork at the magazine, I have been lucky to work with scientists doing some of the most original and groundbreaking work in their fields, whether it concerned astronomy or dinosaurs. Among the scientists I have met were many archaeologists, all of whom impressed me as hardworking people with endless patience and great stories to tell. Chapters in this book grew out of my experience working with these archaeologists on NATIONAL GEOGRAPHIC articles. Much of their research was funded by the National Geographic Society. It should be no surprise then, that I went back to those archaeologists and articles as good sources of information for this book.

While researching this book I came across other sources that were particularly rich with information. I list these here.

Death is a sensitive subject. I know this firsthand because my own mother died when I was seven. I could not think about death, or even look at a cemetery, without crying until I was well into adulthood. In writing this book, I wanted to avoid treading on tender feelings about death that young readers might have. I sought an expert who could guide me regarding what the important messages about death and dying were for young people. I found Linda Goldman, a grief therapist who became a great supporter of this project. Her own book, *Life and Loss: A Guide to Help Grieving Children*, will be very informative for those interested in reading more about this important subject.

Articles in *National Geographic*

First Burials
Gore, Rick. *Dawn of Humans: Neandertals*. January 1996.
Gore, Rick. *Dawn of Humans: People Like Us*. July 2000.

Egypt
Roberts, David. *Age of Pyramids: Egypt's Old Kingdom*. January 1995.
Weeks, Kent. *Valley of the Kings*. September 1998.
Webster, Donovan. *Valley of the Mummies*. October 1999.
Hawass, Zahi. *Egypt's Hidden Tombs*. September 2001.

Scytho-Siberians
Polosmak, Natalya. *A Mummy Unearthed from the Pastures of Heaven*. October 1994.
Edwards, Mike. *Searching for the Scythians*. September 1996.

China
Topping, Audrey. *China's Incredible Find*. August 1978.
Mazzatenta, O. Louis. *A Chinese Emperor's Army for an Eternity*. August 1992.
Mazzatenta, O. Louis. *China's Soldiers Rise from the Earth*. October 1996.
Hessler, Peter. *Treasures of Ancient China*. October 2001.

Moche
Alva, Walter. *Discovering the New World's Richest Tomb*. October 1988.
Donnan, Christopher. *Iconography of the Moche: Unraveling the Mystery of the Warrior-Priest*. October 1988.

Alva, Walter. *New Tomb of Royal Splendor*. June 1990.
Donnan, Christopher. *Masterworks of Art Reveal a Remarkable Pre-Inca World*. June 1990.
Donnan, Christopher. *Moche Burials Uncovered*. March 2001.

Books

Bahn, P., editor. *Tombs, Graves, and Mummies*. Barnes and Noble, New York, 1996.

Bendann, E. *Death Customs: An Analytical Study of Burial Rites*. Alfred A. Knopf, New York, 1930.

Burenhult, G., editor. *People of the Stone Age: Hunter-gatherers and Early Farmers*. American Museum of Natural History. Harper, San Francisco, 1993.

Colman, P. *Corpses, Coffins, and Crypts: A History of Burial*. Henry Holt and Company, New York, 1997.

Habenstein, R. W., and Lamers, W. M. *Funeral Customs the World Over*. The National Funeral Directors Association of the United States, Brookfield, Wisconsin, 1974.

Ikram, S., and Dodson, A. *The Mummy in Ancient Egypt: Equipping the Dead for Eternity*. Thames on Hudson, London, 1998.

Parker Pearson, M. *The Archaeology of Death and Burial*. Texas A & M University Press, College Station, Texas, 2001.

Shreeve, J. *The Neandertal Enigma*. Avon Books, New York, 1995.

Stirland, A. *Human Bones in Archaeology*. Shire Archaeology, Shire Publications, Buckinghamshire, U.K., 1999.

Tattersall, I., and Schwartz, J. *Extinct Humans*. Westview Press, Boulder, Colorado, 2000.

Werner, A. *London Bodies*. Museum of London, London, 1998.

Credits

Cover: Enrico Ferorelli, courtesy Museum of Natural History, Valparaiso, Chile. Back cover: Kenneth Garrett. pg. 1: Bruno Frohlich. pg. 3: Enrico Ferorelli, courtesy Archaeological Museum of San Miguel de Azapa. pg. 4–5: Bruno Frohlich. pg 6: Gordon Wiltsie. pg. 8: James P. Blair. pg. 9: Laura Foreman. pg. 10–11: Roy H. Anderson. pg. 12: Portia Sloan. pg. 13: Chris Sloan, courtesy Dept. of Prehistory and Early Europe, British Museum, London. pg. 14: Kenneth Garrett, courtesy Museum of Prehistory, Mas-d'Azil, France. pg. 16–17: Richard Schlecht. pg. 18: Kenneth Garrett, courtesy Croatian Natural History Museum, Zagreb. pg. 19: Kenneth Garrett, courtesy Vladimir Historical Museum, Russia. pg. 20: Fred Wendorf. Page 21: Bruno Frohlich. pg. 22, top, left to right: Chris Sloan; Kenneth Garrett (see pg. 19); Fred Wendorf; Department of the Ancient Near East, British Museum, London; Enrico Ferorelli, courtesy Museum of Pre-Columbian Art; Patrick Ward. Bottom: Mark Kenoyer. pg. 23, top, left to right: Chris Sloan; Sisse Brimberg; Doug Stern/O. Louis Mazzatenta; Christopher Donnan; Bruno Frohlich; Carol Beckwith and Angela M. Fisher. Bottom: Robert Clark. pg. 24: Portia Sloan. pg. 25: O. Louis Mazzatenta, courtesy Egyptian Museum, Cairo. pg. 26: Chris Sloan, courtesy Department of Egyptian Antiquities, British Museum, London. pg. 27, top: Victor Boswell; bottom: Karl Heinz Hohne, Institute of Mathematics and Computer Science in Medicine, University of Hamburg, Germany (see www.ukekuni-hamburg.de/idv). pg. 28, top: Metropolitan Museum of Art. Bottom: Charles Carter. pg. 29: Chris Klein. pg. 30–31: Kenneth Garrett. pg. 32: Portia Sloan. pg. 33: Sisse Brimberg, courtesy Ukraine Historical Museum, Kiev. pg. 34: Cary Sol Wolinsky, courtesy State Hermitage Museum, St. Petersburg, Russia. pg. 35: Sisse Brimberg, courtesy Ukraine Historic Treasures Museum, Kiev. pg. 36–37: Gregory Manchess. pg. 38, top left: Priit J. Vesilind/National Geographic Society; top right: Charles O'Rear; center right: Bill Bond after Yelena Shumakova. pg. 39: Charles O'Rear. pg. 40: O. Louis Mazzatenta. pg. 41: Portia Sloan. pg. 42–43: Hong Nian Zhang. pg. 43: O. Louis Mazzatenta. pg. 44: Hsien-Min Yang. pg. 45: O. Louis Mazzatenta. pg. 46, left: O. Louis Mazzatenta; right: Wang Bao Ping, courtesy Shaanxi Archaeology Institute. pg. 47: Burt Silverman. pg. 48: Portia Sloan. pg. 49: Kenneth Garrett. pg. 50: Bill Ballenberg. pg. 51: top left, Christopher B. Donnan; top right: Bill Ballenberg; bottom: Martha Cooper. pg. 52–53: Ned Seidler. pg. 54: Kenneth Garrett. pg. 55: Chris Klein. pg. 56: Sisse Brimberg. pg. 57: Jessica Sloan. pg. 58: Photo of Kennewick Man skull, Chip Clark, courtesy of Dr. Douglas Owsley, reconstruction by Keith Kasnot. pg. 59, top: Medford Taylor; center: George Mobley; bottom: Chris Sloan. pg. 60: Carol Beckwith and Angela M. Fisher. pg. 61: George Steinmetz. pg. 62: Laura Foreman. pg. 63: Jessica Sloan. pg. 64: Jodi Cobb.

A toy airplane sits atop a stack of graves in Key West, Florida, where there is not only overcrowding but shallow soil and the regular threat that hurricanes will sweep graves away.

Index

Chinese in Hong Kong visit the graves of their ancestors as part of an ancient tradition on "grave-sweeping day." A family's duty is to sweep the grave, make food offerings, and burn "hell money" for spirits to use in the afterlife.